Copyright © 2020 Ryan & Nissa Andrews

All rights reserved.

Published in the United States by DreamSurf Publishing. Except as permitted under the United States Copyright Act of 1976, no part of this publication may be reproduced or distributed in any form or by any means, or stored in a database or retrieval system, without prior written permission by the publisher.

Andrews, Ryan
Andrews, Nissa
FEARLESS LOVE: MARRIAGE DEVOTIONAL / Ryan & Nissa Andrews – 1st ed.

ISBN 978-0-9983068-3-4

Printed in the United States of America

Design by DreamSurf Studio

FIRST EDITION

We dedicate this devotional to every marriage.
God believes in you. We belive in you.

CONTENTS

00 Intro — 6

01 Fearless Love — 8

02 Love Is Patient — 12

03 Love Is Kind — 16

04 Love Is Not Jealous — 20

05 Love Is Not Proud — 24

06 Love Is Not Rude — 28

07 Love is Not Easily Irritated/Angered — 32

08 Love Keeps No Records of Wrongs — 36

09 Love Rejoices With the Truth — 40

10 Love Bears All Things — 44

11 Love Believes All Things — 48

12 Love Hopes All Things — 52

13 Love Endures All Things — 56

14 Love Never Fails — 60

I Corinthians 13:4-7

Love is patient, love is kind. It does not envy, it does not boast, it is not proud. It does not dishonor others, it is not self-seeking, it is not easily angered, it keeps no record of wrongs. Love does not delight in evil but rejoices with the truth. It always protects, always trusts, always hopes, always perseveres.

00

INTRO

We are so glad you are reading this devotional. The study and application of fearless love saved our marriage and transformed our lives. We are passionate about marriage and want to motivate both men and women around the world to live and respond out of pure love. We started the ministry, Revival Family, for just that purpose. We feel called to help revive marriages.

The next 14 devotions are inspired by our journey with God into fearless love. What does it look like to truly love fearlessly? How do we apply it in our daily lives? What legacy are we leaving behind? Understanding the biblical principles of love will transform not only your marriage but every relationship.

At the end of each devotion, we give an activation. We encourage you to take the time to hear what the Holy Spirit wants to reveal and speak directly to you. If you do this and allow God to show you how to love fearlessly, you will see dramatic results in your marriage. The fruit that you've always longed to see.

- Ryan and Nissa Andrews

THE FIRE

Great marriages are created through God's refining fire, they don't happen accidentally. The purpose is to merge two people into one pure golden relationship.

When gold is heated, impurities come to the surface, but they were there all along. The refining process makes them visible and easier to extract. In the same way, being refined in marriage causes impurities to come out in the open that were there all along. Once they are in the open, then it's easier to remove them and build the marriage of our dreams.

Don't fear the fire; embrace it. It's the fire and refining that causes us to shine like pure gold! How we respond to the refining process determines whether our relationship will be complicated or blissful.

This devotional is an in-depth look into God's perfect example of love. When we love fearlessly, marriage becomes the blessing it was meant to be.

01

FEARLESS LOVE

What is Fearless love? It is free of fear, manipulation, control, anger, strife, chaos and more. Agape love is supernatural, and impacts every area of life, marriage & family. Loving fearlessly means changing our responses to be in alignment with God's plan. Loving without fear creates a space for people to respond appropriately to us.

God is love, there is no fear in love, and our love is perfected each day as we remain in God! This may seem simple, but somehow we get distracted from walking in perfect love. We make choices every day that perfects us in His love and drives out fear (which bears much fruit), or we choose to love like the world in "selfish love," full of fear, (bearing no fruit).

I remember the day we got honest about our choices in how we were loving each other, and it was apparent we weren't bearing "much" fruit. We were bearing some fruit, but when I see where we are today, I can genuinely see the difference. The good news is that God sees us as a finished work, and doesn't pigeon hole us in our struggles and mistakes. He calls out our destiny. It is He who pours grace on our fears and empowers us to walk-in fearless love and freedom. God spoke to our hearts in our moment of honesty and seeking the truth. We listened and did what He said to do. That day completely transformed our marriage.

Fearless love is where we started. If there's no fear in love, why am I responding to my spouse out of fear? We know that when we live in love, we live in God, and He lives in us! This kind of love drives out fear. God completely opened our eyes to see how we were operating under the spirit and influence of fear, which isn't from Him. For God has not given us a spirit of fear; but of power, and of love, and of a sound mind (2 Tim. 1:7).

If you have given your heart to Jesus, you are a new creation, hidden in Christ, and are now partakers of His divine nature. His divine nature is love, for God is love. All who live in God live in love. Now we must choose to walk in it. God has chosen you, appointed, placed, and purposefully planted you so that you wouldn't just bear some fruit but that you would bear much fruit.

Living in love is one of the greatest things you can do in your Christian walk. It honors God, and you will be amazed at how much this will change your perspective and how you treat your spouse. As you read through this devotional, I encourage you to do so with this truth in mind: all who live in love live in God, and God lives in them. There is no fear in love. Once you renew your mind about love and take action, you will begin to walk in fearless love.

NOTES

ACTIVATION

Ask Holy Spirit to show you any areas in your marriage where you may be operating under the spirit and influence of fear.

MEMORY VERSE

God is love, and all who live in love live in God, and God lives in them. And as we live in God, our love grows more perfect. So we will not be afraid on the day of judgment, but we can face him with confidence because we live like Jesus here in this world.

1 John 4:16-17

PRAYER

Lord, thank you that I live in You and You live in me. As we walk together, You are perfecting love in me, and all fear is being driven away. I pray that you will show me what fearless love looks like and give me the grace to walk it out every day. In Jesus' name, amen.

02

LOVE IS PATIENT

"**Love is patient**, love is kind. It does not envy, it does not boast, it is not proud. It does not dishonor others, it is not self-seeking, it is not easily angered, it keeps no record of wrongs. Love does not delight in evil but rejoices with the truth. It always protects, always trusts, always hopes, always perseveres."

1 Corinthians 13:4-7

Getting a complete picture of what "agape love" really is, shifts our perspective. 1 Corinthians 13 is widely understood as the love chapter, and most of us can probably quote at least some of it. "Love is patient, love is kind…"

In the passion translation, 1 Corinthians 13:4 reads, "Love is large and incredibly patient." The same word here in the greek is used throughout the Bible in these ways: "to be of a long spirit, not to lose heart, to persevere patiently and bravely in enduring misfortunes and troubles, to be patient in bearing the offenses and injuries of others, to be mild and slow in avenging, and to be long-suffering.

Loving patiently becomes a tall order when seeing the word in light of its full meaning. It could be said this way, "love is incredibly patient even in difficult relationships." Patient love is persistent love. The kind that says "for better or for worse."

In Aramaic, it can be translated "Love transforms the spirit." I (Ryan) can attest to the transformative power of patiently loving someone through challenging behaviors. Nissa's choice to love me with continual patience was the grace for my freedom.

I had a way of dealing harshly with everyone in the family that didn't sit well with Nissa. When she finaly had the courage to tell me that it was time to change, it wasn't an immediate thing. I had spent 10 years of our marriage acting a certain way, and now I was supposed to instantly be different. That's a tall order for anyone. I wanted to be kind and gentle with my words. I wanted to be the man that she was asking for. However, in certain familiar situations, how I "wanted" to behave didn't always show up. Nonetheless, it was her patience and grace to allow me to regulate myself that empowered me to completely change.

To be honest, I (Nissa) chose to patiently love Ryan, and it wasn't always easy. It can be difficult to choose love when you feel you have been mistreated and hurt. It's frustrating when it doesn't seem like the situation will change in the natural. One of the top things that Ryan says helped him on his journey to change was patient love. So don't lose heart, and don't grow weary in doing good for in due season you will reap a harvest if you don't give up. I can attest to that!

NOTES

ACTIVATION

Ask your spouse for an area that you can show more patience? Then be patient with their response.

MEMORY VERSE

Love is large and incredibly patient.
1 Corinthians 13:4

PRAYER

Lord, thank you for showing me what true love looks like in action. Holy Spirit, teach me how to respond out of patient love towards my spouse every day. I surrender my will to you. In Jesus' name, amen.

03

LOVE IS KIND

"Love is patient, **love is kind**. It does not envy, it does not boast, it is not proud. It does not dishonor others, it is not self-seeking, it is not easily angered, it keeps no record of wrongs. Love does not delight in evil but rejoices with the truth. It always protects, always trusts, always hopes, always perseveres."

1 Corinthians 13:4-7

It seems like a trivial topic of love to talk about kindness, but often the people we are closest to get the worst of us. Kindness is defined as the quality of being friendly, generous, and considerate, but agape kindness is even bigger than that.

Luke chapter six verse thirty-five reads, "But love your enemies, and do good, and lend, expecting nothing in return; and your reward will be great, and you will be sons of the Most High; for He Himself is kind to ungrateful and evil men." Let that sink in a minute. Agape love is being kind regardless of whether people are kind to us or not. When we do that, it's a reflection of the image of God.

It is a choice to be kind. It's harder to make that choice when we feel unappreciated, ignored, or disrespected. In those moments, there is a choice to respond with fear or love. Fear responds with being inconsiderate back. Fearless love responds with kindness and generosity regardless of the actions of the other, expecting nothing in return.

Jesus gave the following illustration, "Can one blind person lead another? Won't they both fall into a ditch?" Trying to combat disrespect with being disrespectful doesn't work. If one person chooses fear and the other person chooses love, then there is hope, and it breaks the fear cycle. If both choose fear, then there will be no end to the pain.

Romans 2:4, "Or do you think lightly of the riches of His

kindness and tolerance and patience, not knowing that the kindness of God leads you to repentance?" Agape love is extravagant in kindness and is meant to melt hearts and create change.

Don't underestimate the power of kindness towards your spouse. If you want to see a real change in your spouse's behavior, you must start with kindness. That leads to true change(repentance). Responding with kindness allows people to reflect on their actions, and then change. This leads to true transformation!

NOTES

ACTIVATION

What act of kindness can I do for my spouse that makes them feel closer to me?

MEMORY VERSE

Or do you think lightly of the riches of His kindness and tolerance and patience, not knowing that the kindness of God leads you to repentance?

Romans 2:4

PRAYER

Lord, You are rich in kindness. I am so grateful for the kindness you continually pour out for me. Help me to respond out of kindness towards my spouse, and make me aware of ways I can show love throughout the day. In Jesus' name, amen.

04

LOVE IS NOT JEALOUS

"Love is patient, love is kind and is **not jealous**; love does not brag and is not arrogant, does not act unbecomingly; it does not seek its own, is not provoked, does not take into account a wrong suffered, does not rejoice in unrighteousness, but rejoices with the truth; bears all things, believes all things, hopes all things, endures all things."

1 Corinthians 13:4-7

This is a big topic for some; Love is not jealous. There are many kinds of jealousy, and all of them create strife in a marriage. Besides the more obvious, one can be jealous of many things, like your partner's achievements or career. Maybe the kids are going through a phase where all they want is one of you more than the other. Envy can creep in and cause a rift in the relationship.

Trust is one of the greatest assets that we have in marriage. The false belief is that trust is earned. In reality, earning trust is manipulation. Inside of fearless love, trust is always given. Forcing someone to earn trust is a form of punishment.

"There is no fear in love, but perfect love casts out fear, because fear has punishment; and the one fearing has not been perfected in love. New American Standard Bible" 1 John 4:8

Fear thinks something like this, "Maybe the kids don't love me anymore since they only want dad right now. Maybe I'm doing something wrong?" Love sees things from a different perspective. It's happy that the kids are connecting with dad.

Regardless of the excuse, it is not loving to be jealous. Love believes all things which we will get into later in the study. We must believe the best of our spouse. We can't allow the enemy to whisper lies to us about their intentions.

Puffing up my chest at every guy that looks at my wife only says to her, "I'm insecure and afraid that I'm not man enough for you."

There is no scenario where a woman feels protected and cherished by a show of force out of jealousy. If I need to flex my alpha male qualities at someone who wants to do harm to my family, that's another story. However, a jealous mind will misread most of these situations.

If your spouse has done things in the past that weren't trustworthy, find a way to trust again. I realize that this is asking a lot for some, but that is what makes this fearless love. There is no fear in love.

If attitudes and behaviors need to shift, then work on that together. Things will not change just because we hope they will. With some issues, it takes work; together-work.

The cause of a jealous heart could be from childhood wounds, marriage hurts, past relationships, or other things. Regardless of the cause, healing the heart and transforming the mind are the main steps toward removing jealously.

Love is not jealous. We are called to love fearlessly.

Doesn't the bible say that He is a jealous God? In the books of Deuteronomy and Exodus where those refrences are found it speaks to God's unwillingness to share us with other gods in reference to idolatry.

In First Corinthians the word is " zēloō", which referrs to behavior. It could be read, "Love is not heated and doesn't boil with envy, hatred or anger."

ACTIVATION

Jealousy hurts your relationship and limits your love. If this is a struggle, ask yourself, "why?" Prayerfully consider your heart in all situations surrounding your spouse.

If there is a real reason for lack of trust, then find someone to help you deal with it now. Don't wait!

MEMORY VERSE

'For where envy and self-seeking exist, confusion and every evil thing are there."
James 3:16

PRAYER

Lord, give me a humble heart. Teach me to walk in fearless love, free of any envy, strife, or jealousy. Lead me into truth. In Jesus' name, amen.

05

LOVE IS NOT PROUD

"Love is patient, love is kind. It does not envy, it does not boast, it **is not proud**. It does not dishonor others, it is not self-seeking, it is not easily angered, it keeps no record of wrongs. Love does not delight in evil but rejoices with the truth. It always protects, always trusts, always hopes, always perseveres."

1 Corinthians 13:4-7

Pride is the reason for most quarrels and conflicts that we have with one another. *What is the cause of your conflicts and quarrels with each other? Doesn't the battle begin inside of you as you fight to have your own way and fulfill your own desires? James 4:1(PT)*

Opposition and resistance in our marriage are usually the products of pride. The cure for this is humility. Pride demands its own way, but exits when humility enters! Humility also ushers in grace.

> "God resists the proud, But gives grace to the humble."
> James 4:6

One of the things that frustrated Ryan most was that I (Nissa) rarely apologized. This was something I wasn't aware of at the time and shocked me when he finally told me how he felt about it. In fact, being an inward processor, I began thinking to myself how that wasn't true. I went into denial and instantly blamed him. No, that's not me, you're the one who never apologizes, I thought to myself. Both reactions stem from pride. When you are honest with your responses and thoughts of the heart, it becomes easier to see. The only way out was humility. It was time to own my part of the equation, humble myself, and express how sorry I was. I didn't apologize to appease my husband, I apologized because I saw the error of my ways and my actions needed to change.

LET US LOOK AT THE DIFFERENT WAYS THAT LOVE AND PRIDE RESPOND...

"Love listens; pride talks. Love forgives; pride resents. Love gives; pride takes. Love apologizes; pride blames. Love understands; pride assumes. Love accepts; pride rejects. Love trusts; pride doubts. Love asks; pride demands. Love leads; pride drives. Love frees up; pride binds up. Love builds up; pride tears down. Love encourages; pride discourages. Love confronts; pride is passive-aggressive or aggressive-aggressive. Love is peaceful; pride is fearful. Love clarifies with truth; pride confuses with lies. Love and pride are mutually exclusive. Love dies with pride but comes alive with humility." -unknown

ACTIVATION

What is an area of your life where you always insist on your own way? Find a way to change any unrealistic expectations today.

MEMORY VERSE

God resists the proud but gives grace to the humble.

James 4:6

PRAYER

Lord, I repent of pride and demanding my own way. Open my eyes to see the areas in which I am walking in pride. I humble myself before you and am grateful for the grace you give that is divine empowerment to change. In Jesus' name, amen.

06

LOVE IS NOT RUDE

"Love suffers long and is kind; love does not envy; love does not parade itself, is not puffed up; **does not behave rudely**, does not seek its own, is not provoked, thinks no evil; does not rejoice in iniquity, but rejoices in the truth; bears all things, believes all things, hopes all things, endures all things."

1 Corinthians 13:4-7

Love does not dishonor others. It doesn't act unbecomingly and is not rude. Rudeness refers to words or actions that are offensive, hurtful, or embarrassing to others. Rudeness is impolite and disrespectful. Often in marriages, rudeness is disguised as honesty, openness, or truth. You know the saying," I'm not being rude, I'm just being honest." What your saying may have truth in it, but there is a way to be honest and open without being disrespectful, hurtful, and mean. Without love, you are just a clanging cymbal, and it will be hard to hear anything you have to say.

I (Ryan) never thought that my words or actions were rude. One of Nissa's issues was how I embarrassed her in public with my behavior. Part of that was my issue, and part was her issue. One way to show her love was to be honoring and considerate. I (Nissa) wasn't rude with my words, but with my actions. How I quietly behaved communicated disrespect to Ryan. An example of that would be in disciplining the children. Ryan had his way, and if I didn't like how it was done, I would go to the children and fix it in my own way. How I went about it was rude, dishonoring, and disrespectful to Ryan. We were both in the habit of some rude behaviors. They looked different from one another but were rude nonetheless. The beautiful thing is that once you realize what you are doing and how it is affecting your spouse, making the necessary changes are simple. It just takes being intentional with our choices and actions until we form a new habit. Walking in love will become the new natural.

Kindness is an excellent antidote to rudeness. Kindness shows self-discipline, especially when confronted with someone rude. If you combat rudeness with being disrespectful back, you continue to breed disconnection and lack of love. Being rude is a choice, but so is kindness. Always choose love! Love is gentle and consistently kind to all and is not rude.

When you speak healing words, you offer others fruit from the tree of life. But unhealthy, negative words do nothing but crush their hopes.
Proverbs 15:4 (Passion Translation)

NOTES

ACTIVATION

Would other people describe me as a courteous and considerate person? What about your spouse or someone close to you? Would he or she describe you this way? Is that what your children would say of you?

MEMORY VERSE

Lovers of God think before they speak, but the careless blurt out wicked words meant to cause harm.

Proverbs 15:28

PRAYER

Lord, thank you for Your refining fire that purifies my heart, motives, and responses. Holy Spirit, help me to think before I speak, and I pray that my words and actions would always be loving and never rude. Open my eyes to see any areas that my words or actions are rude towards my spouse. In Jesus' name, amen.

07

LOVE IS NOT EASILY ANGERED

"Love is patient, love is kind. It does not envy, it does not boast, it is not proud. It does not dishonor others, it is not self-seeking, **it is not easily angered**, it keeps no record of wrongs. Love does not delight in evil but rejoices with the truth. It always protects, always trusts, always hopes, always perseveres."

1 Corinthians 13:4-7

When anger was a real struggle for me (Ryan), it felt very rational. I was shocked at how hard it was for other people to see just how bad they were upsetting me. I mean, if you see someone getting angry, shouldn't you just back off so they can calm down? I blamed everyone else, and at the heart of things, I was a victim. My emotional state was a slave to how other people behaved. After all, I believed that I was just made this way.

The excuse was that I wore my heart on my sleeve, so whatever was inside showed on the outside. I wrongly assumed that people who didn't express their anger like me were just hiding it. I believed that I was taking the high road by being open. The truth is that anger is a tool that I chose to use, so I would be heard. And I was always irritated.

Irritation is a good indicator that you are taking something personally. Since love is not easily angered, then someone with a short fuse is not showing love. Love is patient. Anger itself is not sinful but can quickly lead to sinful expressions.

"He who is slow to anger is better than the mighty, and he who rules his spirit than he who takes a city." Proverbs 16:32

"People with understanding control their anger; a hot temper shows great foolishness." Proverbs 14: 29

"My dearest brothers and sisters, take this to heart: Be quick to listen, but slow to speak. And be slow to become angry, for human anger is never a legitimate tool to promote God's righteous purpose."

James 1:19-20

As we see from scripture, anger and irritation are both foolish and ineffective. So, how do we get better at controlling our anger and irritation? The prophet Joel shows us where it starts!

So rend your heart, and not your garments; Return to the Lord your God, For He is gracious and merciful, slow to anger, and of great kindness; and He relents from doing harm.

Joel 2:13

Joel's prophetic message here is to repent with a genuine and sincere change of heart. Real repentance is not just feeling sorry about your actions, but having a complete change of heart, and a complete change of heart requires more than a partial surrender.

The key to eliminating frustration, irritation, and anger is to literally change your mind. I had to change my thoughts towards my wife and kids. When the kids were wild and "driving me nuts," I had to tell myself how cute they were. When it felt like my wife was ignoring me, I chose to believe that she was overwhelmed and needed my help. This is what repentance looks like in a practical sense.

If you struggle with negative expressions of anger (like I did), then make an action plan for dealing with emotions before anything sets you off. Then keep at it until everything lines up. If you need help, reach out to someone. Resolving the anger issue is a massive step forward in having a beautiful relationship.

ACTIVATION

What are your top two or three irritations? Change your mind about them right now, so when they happen again, you will have a plan with how to deal with it.

MEMORY VERSE

The Lord is compassionate and gracious, slow to anger, abounding in love.

Psalm 103:8

PRAYER

Lord, I repent for anger and irritation. Transform my mind to be like yours. Open my eyes to see things the way that you see them. In Jesus' name, amen.

08

LOVE KEEPS NO RECORDS OF WRONGS

"Love is patient, love is kind. It does not envy, it does not boast, it is not proud. It does not dishonor others, it is not self-seeking, it is not easily angered, **it keeps no record of wrongs**. Love does not delight in evil but rejoices with the truth. It always protects, always trusts, always hopes, always perseveres."

1 Corinthians 13:4-7

We are quick to say I love you, but how often does the scorecard come out as soon as someone gets angry? Here comes the list of all the ways we have been wronged! Accusations fly, and painful memories are often brought up. However, this is not how Agape love responds. Agape love forgives and refuses to keep a record of all the wrongs.

Jesus, our beautiful savior, thankfully doesn't keep a list of our failures. Instead, He prayed, "Father, forgive them for they know not what they do," as he was dying a brutal death on the cross.

> *"For I will forgive their wickedness*
> *and will remember their sins no more."*
> *Hebrews 8:12*

If you don't remember the sins, you won't be able to bring them up. This seems to be the hardest thing for people to do. An offended heart doesn't easily forget. When we refuse to release another for a pain that they have inflicted on us, then we only bring greater anguish on ourselves. Read the Parable of the Unforgiving Servant in Matthew 18: 21-35 for a deeper understanding of unlimited forgiveness.

If we have been forgiven at an infinite proportion, how then do we dare to hold a wrong against someone else and punish them? If a perfect God has forgiven us for so much, how can we not forgive our spouse?

In the practical, unforgiveness looks like: withholding love, withholding sex, sarcastic comments, putting your own needs first, hurtful digs, ignoring each other, selfishness, fighting over little things, holding each other to the fire, making your spouse prove themselves trustworthy, etc. Harboring unforgiveness can result in fear, anxiety, depression, insomnia, and other soul torturing issues. All this, because of a scorecard!

None of this refers to pretending as though there is nothing wrong. We must deal with issues as they come up. Love teaches us to speak the truth kindly, and deal with our hurts; then let them go forever.

An excellent way to see if you have erected a wall against your spouse is this question, "Do I feel differently toward them?" If you are feeling angry, bitter or something else, then give it to Jesus and talk openly with your spouse about it. A discussion filled with fearless love will pull your hearts back together.

NOTES

ACTIVATION

Get rid of your score sheet. Make a list privately of any and all areas that you are offended, angry, irritated, and disappointed in your spouse. After you have written it down, if there is anything that needs to be discussed, now is a good time. Then forgive them, rip up the list, and remember it no more.

MEMORY VERSE

For I will forgive their wickedness and will remember their sins no more.
Hebrews 8:12

PRAYER

Lord, I'm no longer keeping a score sheet for_____. Help me love_____ like you love them, unconditionally and no strings attached. Help me to forgive easily every day moving forward and convict me quickly if I'm falling once again into the trap of keeping score. In Jesus' name, amen.

09

LOVE REJOICES WITH TRUTH

"Love is patient, love is kind. It does not envy, it does not boast, it is not proud. It does not dishonor others, it is not self-seeking, it is not easily angered, it keeps no record of wrongs. **Love does not delight in evil but rejoices with the truth**. It always protects, always trusts, always hopes, always perseveres."

1 Corinthians 13:4-7

Love joyfully celebrates honesty because it finds no delight in what is wrong. Even when honesty doesn't feel great, we are supposed to celebrate our spouse sharing what's on their heart. When Nissa felt safe enough to use her voice to tell me how I was treating her, it wasn't easy to hear. Even hearing the words, "I don't feel safe…" can hurt. But, as lovers, there is no delight in what is wrong. How can we celebrate our marriage when one person isn't free to use their voice and share what isn't feeling right to them.

When Ryan shared that I lived my life not trusting him (having trust issues), I didn't initially celebrate the honesty. However, I found no delight in my wrongdoing. I repented and changed my actions that day forward. Today I can say with absolute certainty that I celebrate that day of honesty. Why? Because honesty transformed our marriage.

No one likes to be wrong, and when our spouse calls us out, it can feel like an attack. But if we listen to what they are saying to us through the filter of supernatural agape love, it becomes easier to celebrate them. Rejoice with the truth that both of you were created by God for such a time as this. Abba brought you together to refine one another. When the truth is spoken, it doesn't always come the way we initially would like to receive it. Don't let that deter you from receiving the truth. Let the Truth set you free!

The goal of love is connection. When people feel unloved, disrespected, dishonored, unheard, devalued, unseen, etc. they tend to respond poorly. That doesn't take away from any truth that might be trying to make its way to our hearts. When things are not going well, it's common to dwell on each other's poor behaviors. It can even become a point of conversation with friends and confidants. We end up seeing their faults in just about everything they do. When you find yourself falling into this pattern, intentionally shift your thoughts and begin to dwell on the good things and celebrate the small wins. "Whatever things are true, whatever things are noble, whatever things are just, whatever things are pure, whatever things are lovely, whatever things are of good report, if there is any virtue and if there is anything praiseworthy-meditate on these things." Philippians 4:8.

Let go of expectations, and give each other grace while you are making the necessary changes. Rejoice in the truth of who God made your spouse to be. And why He brought you together, to begin with. As we take joy in our spouse, even in the simple things, it opens our eyes to see how to communicate better.

A helpful tip is to take those moments of being honest with one another to the secret place with the Father and let Truth set you free. Lay those conversations at the feet of your Daddy (Abba). Ask Holy Spirit to guide you into all truth and teach you how to walk in freedom and victory in every area of your relationship with your spouse.

I (Nissa) did this many times. I took my fears, my pain, my marriage struggles with Ryan to the secret place with the Father. It was fascinating to me that each time, Abba redirected my focus off of my husband, and on to me and HIM! Every time He filled me with supernatural love and responses to take into my marriage. God transformed my perspective, my actions, and the way I loved and responded to Ryan. He taught me how to see Ryan, as He sees him, and how to call forth his destiny. God sees Ryan as a finished work, not the way I see him at the moment. These times were so empowering, full of truth, grace, and loads of mercy.

ACTIVATION

Make a list of your spouse's qualities the way that God sees them.

MEMORY VERSE

"If you abide in My word, you are My disciples indeed. And you shall know the truth, and the truth shall make you free."

John 8:31-32

PRAYER

Lord, thank you for truth; I rejoice in it. I find no delight in what is wrong. I open my heart to continually hear and receive truth over my life. Holy Spirit, teach me how to apply the truth, so I can walk in complete freedom and get every breakthrough I need for my marriage. In Jesus' name, amen.

10
LOVE BEARS ALL THINGS

"Love is patient, love is kind and is not jealous; love does not brag and is not arrogant, does not act unbecomingly; it does not seek its own, is not provoked, does not take into account a wrong suffered, does not rejoice in unrighteousness, but rejoices with the truth; **bears all things**, believes all things, hopes all things, endures all things."

1 Corinthians 13:4-7

In the passion translation, it says it this way, "Love is a safe place of shelter." The word used in the Greek is "to conceal the errors and faults of others, or to cover." Uncovering one another is one of the most destructive actions that we can do. Our spouse is supposed to be a safe place and should protect our vulnerabilities from the world. If we are to be a safe place, why is it that we often attack instead of protect. Why do we expose rather than cover one another? Love bears all; it does not bare all. Criticizing, complaining, vilifying, and pointing out your spouse's faults to others not only tears them down, but it demolishes your own house (place of shelter). This is not loving. A "safe place of shelter" means we are protected from within the walls and from the outside elements. We are to protect and cover each other no matter what storms come.

Here's a quick made-up story about uncovering. Imagine you need to find a restroom quick. You're at a busy café, and there's a bit of a line. Finally, it's your turn, you rush in and sit on the throne. Looking up at the door, you realize that in haste, you have forgotten to lock the door. It's a single-use, co-ed restroom, and fear has started to creep in. Standing up to lock the door is no longer an option, so you're praying that you make it through before someone tries to come in. The door handle starts to turn, and the potential fear changes to embarrassing terror. The color drains from your face as the door is flung wide open by your spouse. They are pointing and laughing and showing everyone in the café this incredibly vulnerable and shameful moment. The terror turns to rage, and a gaping heart wound has just opened up. If it was some random stranger, it would be bad enough, but from the one who is supposed to protect and guard the door is what makes it more wounding.

Love won't uncover each other to friends and family. We all have struggles and don't always get things right. Using family and close friends as confidants for the struggles in our marriage is not a great idea. We say this because not only are we uncovering our spouse, but we are passing down an offense. Even if the two of you reconcile and you see a breakthrough in your places of struggle, there may be permanent damage done with the people that you uncovered your spouse to. They may not see your spouse the same ever again. Do not take this topic lightly.

We are not suggesting that you keep silent. By all means, talk with people who can help. The point is to not be loose with your tongue. There is a different heart behind someone who is upset at their spouse and is looking for pity, agreement, and comfort as opposed to someone who is looking for wisdom, truth, and help. Use wisdom and ask God to show you with whom you can confide in that is also a safe place.

Agape love finds a way to conceal the errors and faults of our spouse until they can change. Once again, this is not permission to ignore issues. It's important to discuss shortcomings and grow into the person that we need to be for each other. Inside of love, issues are together-problems to work on. In the process of going through the marriage fire, we must strive to not damage one another. Love bears all things.

ACTIVATION

Does your love bear all things? Where do you find it the hardest to bear all things in your marriage?

MEMORY VERSE

"Above all, keep fervent in your love for one another, because love covers a multitude of sins."

1 Peter 4:8

PRAYER

Lord, give me a deeper understanding of what it means to truly bear all things. Strengthen our marriage and help to make us into a safe place of shelter for one another. In Jesus' name, amen.

11
LOVE BELIEVES ALL THINGS

"Love is patient, love is kind and is not jealous; love does not brag and is not arrogant, does not act unbecomingly; it does not seek its own, is not provoked, does not take into account a wrong suffered, does not rejoice in unrighteousness, but rejoices with the truth; bears all things, **believes all things**, hopes all things, endures all things."

1 Corinthians 13:4-7

We all long for someone who will believe the best about us, and who brings out the best in us even in our worst moments. God does that and how beautiful it is!! No matter what we do and how bad things get messed up, we are assured of His love. That is because fearless love believes all things.

This is what we are called to do in our marriage. We need to believe in our spouse. We can think the best about them once we have believed the truth about who we are to Jesus. He believes the best of us! Freely you have received, freely give. We can't do this in our own strength or apart from Jesus. If we try to do it based on sheer willpower, we will eventually come to the end of our own strength. It's time to strengthen yourself in the Lord and remind yourself what God thinks about you and your spouse, then you will have an abundance of goodness to give away.

It's so easy to see failures and weaknesses in one another, but it's much better to see the best in each other! Meditate on what is good. Likewise, complaining may be more comfortable than believing the best. Still, fearless love speaks the best over each other rather than pointing out the negatives. It assumes that their intentions are true even if they fail and believes that they want to do better, and to be everything that God made them. Ask God to show you how He sees your spouse when it's difficult to see the best. Perspective changes our actions towards one another.

Love is always willing to risk giving others the benefit of the doubt because it sees the best. Believing the best is not about ignoring your spouse's faults, but more about recognizing that they desire to become more than they currently are. Just as God sees us as a finished work, that is how fearless love sees your spouse.

Don't forget that God sees your marriage as a finished work too. He believes the very best for the two of you. He knows that you have what it takes to have a golden marriage. God brought the two of you together and believes in you completely. God is for you!!

NOTES

ACTIVATION

If Jesus were looking out through my eyes, how would He see my spouse? How would you treat your spouse from this perspective?

MEMORY VERSE

"For by one offering He has perfected forever those who are being sanctified."

Hebrews 10:14

PRAYER

Lord, thank you for always believing the best in us. Your sacrificial love has made us perfect forever! Help me to see my spouse from this perspective. Help me to always believe the best in my spouse and open my eyes to see them the way you see them. Give me the grace to fearlessly love them. In Jesus' name, amen.

12

LOVE HOPES ALL THINGS

"Love is patient, love is kind and is not jealous; love does not brag and is not arrogant, does not act unbecomingly; it does not seek its own, is not provoked, does not take into account a wrong suffered, does not rejoice in unrighteousness, but rejoices with the truth; bears all things, believes all things, **hopes all things**, endures all things."

1 Corinthians 13:4-7

12 Love Hopes All Things 53

Hope is the expectation that something good is going to happen. The word hope here in Greek means to trust or expect. Hope looks to the future with total confidence, expectation, and trust because our future is good. How can we say that with unwavering confidence? Let's allow this truth to sink in. "All things work together for good to those who love God and are called according to His purpose." Romans 8:28 This scripture states that everything will work out for our good! Now that's good news!

The failure to hope all things is unbelief. It's unbelief in the nature of God's work. It's unbelief that God finishes what he starts. He doesn't walk away or quit on us. Abba is a finisher.

Being confident of this very thing, that He who has begun a good work in you will complete it until the day of Jesus Christ;

Philippians 1:6

A love that hopes all things is a love that never gives up on each other. Here are a few examples of what not hoping in all things looks like in marriage.

1) Writing your spouse off as a lost cause.

2) Pushing your spouse out of your life.

3) Moving on in your heart.

Losing hope can be silent and deadly to your marriage. You can choose to be a victim, or you can choose to maintain control, and that choice is based on your perception.

> *"Your **eye** is like a lamp that provides light for your body. When your **eye** is healthy, your whole body is filled with light. But when your **eye** is unhealthy, your whole body is filled with darkness. And if the light you think you have is actually darkness, how deep that darkness is!*
> *Matthew 6:22-23*

Our eye is how we perceive things. Re-read the verse putting the word "perception" in place of the word "eye."

In short, your attitude is affected by the way you perceive things. If your perception is unhealthy, you will slowly choke out all hope. Unhealthy perception is the silent killer of hope.

To hope all things, we must believe all things. When we believe all things, it becomes more natural to expect good things for our future. If you find yourself losing hope, it's a great indicator that you need an adjustment in your perception.

Go back to the drawing board of believing all things. Lacking joy is another indicator that you are losing hope. When perception changes, then attitude and responses also change. This creates an atmosphere of great joy and the freedom to respond differently!

ACTIVATION

What are 3 future dreams you have together as a couple?

MEMORY VERSE

Now may the God of hope fill you with all joy and peace in believing, that you may abound in hope by the power of the Holy Spirit.

Romans 15:13

PRAYER

Lord, thank you that you are the God of hope and that I abound in hope by the power of the Holy Spirit. I expect that something good is going to happen. Help me shift my perception and always see things this way. I choose to look to the future of my marriage with total confidence, expectation, and trust, knowing that our future together is good. In Jesus' name, amen.

13
LOVE ENDURES ALL THINGS

"Love is patient, love is kind and is not jealous; love does not brag and is not arrogant, does not act unbecomingly; it does not seek its own, is not provoked, does not take into account a wrong suffered, does not rejoice in unrighteousness, but rejoices with the truth; bears all things, believes all things, hopes all things, **endures all things**."

1 Corinthians 13:4-7

13 Love Endures All Things

We all want a love who will never give up on us. We long for someone who will stick by us in the good and the bad. The trouble is we don't always want to be that person. Enduring love is something that you do. It's a choice, and you must choose to remain committed.

Love always perseveres. It remains; it abides. Abiding means that you stay connected. When you stay connected, you will bear much fruit. We can't do this apart from God. If you want an enduring love, you must first abide in the True Vine, for He is the source of enduring love. You can't give away what you do not possess.

"Abide in Me, and I in you. As the branch cannot bear fruit of itself, unless it abides in the vine, neither can you, unless you abide in Me.

I am the vine; you are the branches. He who abides in Me, and I in him, bears much fruit; for without Me you can do nothing. If you abide in Me, and My words abide in you, you will ask what you desire, and it shall be done for you. By this My Father is glorified, that you bear much fruit; so you will be My disciples. "As the Father loved Me, I also have loved you; abide in My love. If you keep My commandments, you will abide in My love, just as I have kept My Father's commandments and abide in His love.

These things I have spoken to you, that My joy may remain in you, and that your joy may be full. This is My commandment, that you love one another as I have loved you. Greater love has no one than this, than to lay down one's life for his friends." - John 15: 4-5, 7-13

Love is a choice. It is an action, and is sacrificial; love looks like something. Enduring-love is the heart of what love does. All the attributes of love that we've covered so far in this devotional shows us how love endures.

I know that giving up sometimes seems more natural than sticking it out, but fearless love never gives up. Love endures through every circumstance. In fact, during the hardest of times, that's when fearless love becomes most visible in us. How will the world know that we are followers of Jesus if our love gives up on each other, calls it quits, and doesn't endure? The world gives love based on how they feel, but not those who abide in agape love. Agape love is sacrificial; it lays its life down for each other and loves fearlessly regardless of feelings.

Enduring-love brings joy! The lie the enemy wants us to believe is that enduring-love is not joyful. I know what you were thinking as you were reading about enduring-love; it doesn't sound very pleasant or enjoyable. Notice what Jesus tells his disciples regarding love that abides. He says, "these things I have spoken to you, that My joy may remain in you, and that your joy may be full." The promise is that His joy would remain in you and makes your joy complete. You will have joy because enduring-love bears much fruit.

"And let us not grow weary while doing good, for in due season we shall reap if we do not lose heart."

Galatians 6:9

ACTIVATION

Have you made the decision to never give up on your spouse? Is your love faithful and enduring? Choose it today!

MEMORY VERSE

The Lord is good, and His faithful love endures forever; His faithfulness continues through all generations.

Psalm 100:5

PRAYER

Lord, thank you for Your enduring faithful love that has no end. As I abide in you, I pray that I would endure and that my enduring love would bear much fruit in my marriage. I am grateful that as I ask what I desire, it is done for me because I abide in You and Your words. In Jesus' name, amen.

14

LOVE NEVER FAILS

"Love never fails."
1 Corinthians 13:8

Love is victorious!! Fearless, agape love is the victory plan for your marriage. Love never fails to bring freedom and is meant to release you from feeling burden or shame. It doesn't mean that every action you make is perfect from here on out.

Sometimes our demonstration of love fails, but that doesn't mean that love itself fails. A perfect example is the Apostle Peter. Peter was convinced that he loved Jesus and would stand by him through thick and thin. He told Jesus that he would never deny him, and then hours later, he did just that.

Peter responded out of fear at that moment instead of love. He was distraught over what he had done and thought he ruined his future relationship with Jesus. All hope was lost.

That is until Jesus came to Peter and restored him through fearless, unfailing, patient, enduring, holding no record of wrongs kind of love. He restored him and gave him a purpose. Jesus told Peter to feed His sheep.

God doesn't see our failures; He sees our potential. Unfailing-love empowered Peter to rise to the occasion and to become all that Jesus knew him to be. Peter went from denying Jesus to dying for him. How? Because love never fails.

We can learn so much from the story of Peter's restoration. In our moments of failure, let the source of unfailing love invite you in and restore you. You may have failed once or twice, but it doesn't mean that you can't get it right. You have what it takes. Get up and try again.

Don't give up because God is ready and is present at all times to pull you out of your shame, disappointments, and failures. He will fill you with everything that you need to walk in fearless love. Love is victorious over every failure.

Love never fails!

ACTIVATION

Take your failures and your shame to Jesus? Let him restore you and give you purpose once again.

MEMORY VERSE

Let the morning bring me word of your unfailing love, for I have put my trust in you. Show me the way I should go, for to you I entrust my life.

Psalm 143:8

PRAYER

Lord, thank you for Your unfailing love. Restore to me the joy of my salvation! Holy Spirit, I surrender all my failures to you. I choose to walk in unfailing love and declare that we will have a victorious marriage. In Jesus' name, amen.

WE BELIEVE IN YOU!

Operating in fearless love is simple, but also challenging. It challenges us to love like Jesus in all circumstances. We cannot do it in our human strength, but with Jesus, all things are possible. As you walk out this journey of treating each other differently, remember grace and mercy are God's tools for change.

SUPPORT REVIVAL FAMILY BY SOWING

We have a big vision for marriages! It's our heart to facilitate healthy relationships and families. We started Revival Family for just that purpose, to create life-shifting training, support, and encouragement.

A lot of the marriages that need this message are not looking for it. You can create change by putting a copy of this devotional into their hands. Or better yet, start a 14-week marriage group and do the study together. Go to our website and get your group kit at **RevivalFam.com**

We have more resources for marriage, family, men, and women at our website **RevivalFam.com**.
- Marriage Revival Encounters
- Godmade Men
- Supernatural Pain-Free Childbirth
- Follow Us on Social Media

www.ingramcontent.com/pod-product-compliance
Lightning Source LLC
LaVergne TN
LVHW051528070426
835507LV00023B/3371